Mike Trout

By Jon M. Fishman

AMAZING
ATHLETES

Lerner Publications Company • Minneapolis

Lerner Publications Company
A division of Lerner Publishing Group, Inc.
241 First Avenue North
Minneapolis, MN 55401 USA

For reading levels and more information, look up this title at www.lernerbooks.com.

Library of Congress Cataloging-in-Publication Data

Fishman, Jon M.
    Mike Trout / by Jon M. Fishman.
        pages   cm. — (Amazing athletes)
    Includes index.
    ISBN 978–1–4677–2142–4 (lib. bdg. : alk. paper)
    ISBN 978–1–4677–2437–1 (eBook)
    1. Trout, Mike, 1991—Juvenile literature. 2. Baseball players—United States—Biography—
Juvenile literature. I. Title.
    GV865.T73F57 2014
    796.357092—dc23 [B]   2013036155

Manufactured in the United States of America
1 – BP – 12/31/13

TABLE OF CONTENTS

Mike hits a fly ball toward left field in a game against the Seattle Mariners.

"ONE OF THOSE NIGHTS"

Los Angeles Angels outfielder Mike Trout walked back to the **dugout**. The day was May 21, 2013. Mike's first at bat had not gone well. He had just struck out against the Seattle Mariners.

Mike is one of the most exciting players in Major League Baseball (MLB). He won the **Rookie** of the Year award in 2012. He also finished second to Detroit's Miguel Cabrera for the **American League (AL)** Most Valuable Player (MVP) award that year.

In the third inning, Mike stepped up to bat again. He swung at a tough pitch.

Mike winds up for a swing.

Mike drops his bat after smashing the ball to the outfield.

Mike became just the seventh player in Angels history to hit for the cycle.

The ball bounced weakly to the right side of the infield. Mike raced to first base. He is one of the fastest runners in baseball. It was going to be close. Safe! Mike had a **single**.

In the fourth inning, Mike smashed the ball to right field. It bounced against the outfield wall. Mike sped around the bases for a **triple**. Two innings later, he crushed a pitch to the outfield for a **double**. He was on fire!

The crowd buzzed when Mike came to bat in the eighth inning. They wanted to see if he could complete the cycle. A cycle is a rare feat in baseball. No Angels player had done it since 2006. Mike already had a single, a double, and a triple. All he needed to complete the cycle was a **home run**.

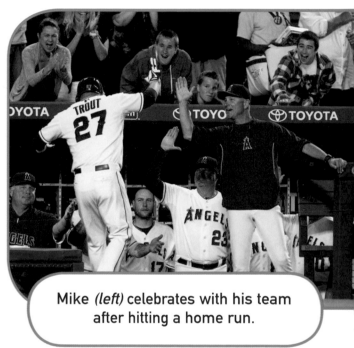

Mike *(left)* celebrates with his team after hitting a home run.

Seattle's pitcher threw the ball. Mike swung with all his might. He launched the ball high and deep. It sailed through the night sky and over the outfield wall. Home run! The Angels had a huge lead, 12–0.

The crowd stood on their feet and cheered as Mike ran around the bases. His teammates surrounded him and gave him high fives. "It was just one of those nights," Mike said later. "It feels great." His mother was also excited. "One proud Mama!!" she wrote on Twitter. "TROUTSTANDING!!!"

Mike had a passion for baseball long before he joined the major leagues.

FAMILY BUSINESS

Mike was born in Vineland, New Jersey, on August 7, 1991. He grew up in nearby Millville. Great baseball players usually come from places that are warm most of the year.

Many children give Wiffle ball a try before they learn to play baseball.

In states such as Florida, young players can practice their baseball skills even in the winter. But New Jersey winters are cold and snowy.

Mike's parents are named Jeff and Debbie. He has a sister, Teal, and a brother, Tyler. Mike's father also played professional baseball. He toiled in the Minnesota Twins **minor-league** system from 1983 to 1986. Jeff admits his son is a better player than he was. "[Mike's] bigger, faster, stronger," Jeff said.

Wiffle ball is similar to baseball. A Wiffle ball is made of plastic and covered with holes. A Wiffle ball bat is also made of plastic.

"I was just a small guy who had to work for everything I got."

The Trout family knew right away that Mike would be a good athlete. He took to baseball very easily. The family used to play Wiffle ball in their backyard. "Mikey used to beat us all the time," said Teal. "He'd get up and we wouldn't even try to get him out. He was always the best hitter, and always the fastest."

Jeff Trout played baseball too. He taught Mike all he knew about the game.

Mike loved baseball from the beginning. He wanted to play catch all the time. Sometimes he would sleep in his uniform after youth games. Jeff thought his son had a chance to be a special player.

Jeff had become a high school history teacher after he finished playing baseball. Jeff works at Millville High School. He is also one

Millville is a small city in New Jersey.

of the coaches for the school's baseball and football teams.

Jeff brought Mike to baseball practice every day. Mike caught balls in the outfield. During games, he served as the team's **ball boy**. "He basically grew up in the locker room," Jeff said. Mike was already a polished baseball player by the time he was ready for high school.

Mike was one of the best athletes in his high school.

LIKE A THUNDERBOLT

Mike's baseball coaches at Millville High School didn't waste any time. They put Mike on the **varsity** team his freshman year. Most first-year students start at a lower level. But Mike welcomed the challenge. His strength and speed wowed his teammates.

Many athletes are fast and strong. But Mike had learned from his father that he would still have to work hard to be his best. "[Jeff] knew all the hard work that goes into it and you could tell that had been ingrained in Mike, too," said a **scout**.

In addition to baseball, Mike played football and basketball in high school.

Mike played **shortstop** for the Millville Thunderbolts. He also pitched. By the time he was a junior, he was one of the best pitchers in the state.

Mike *(top center)* liked to play basketball when baseball season was over.

In 2008, he won eight games and lost only two. He also hit nine home runs as a batter. His **batting average** was .530. Mike was named to the All-State team as one of the best players in New Jersey.

Mike worked hard to be a good athlete and student in high school.

In 2009, the Thunderbolts moved Mike to the outfield. His power and running ability helped make the move easy. "Mike has top-of-the-line speed in a **linebacker's** body," said one of his coaches.

The senior blasted 18 home runs, a state record. He became a member of the All-State team for the second time.

Scouts had been watching Mike for a long time. Some of them thought he could be a great MLB player. But others weren't so sure. Players from northern states such as New Jersey often don't make it to the major leagues.

Los Angeles Angels scout Greg Morhardt knows that scouts sometimes overlook northern players. "That's where you can steal a kid," Morhardt said. He wanted Mike. "I'd never seen a seventeen-year-old who was that fast and strong," the scout said.

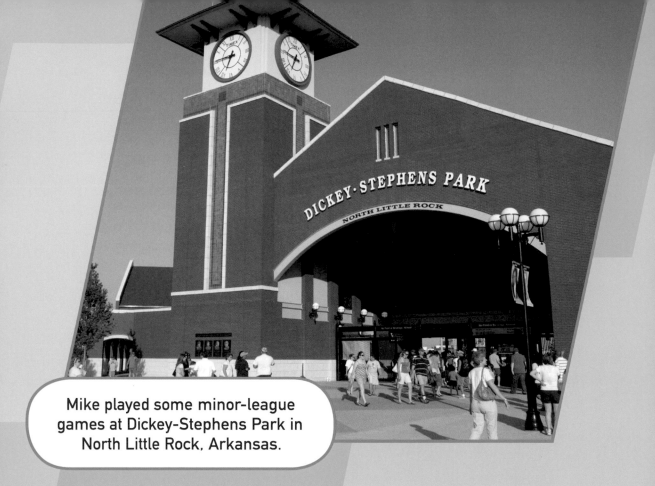

Mike played some minor-league games at Dickey-Stephens Park in North Little Rock, Arkansas.

MAJOR-LEAGUE THRILL

The MLB held its 2009 **draft** on June 9. Most people agreed that pitcher Stephen Strasburg would be the first choice. The Angels thought Mike was the second-best player in the draft. But most teams would get to pick before Los Angeles took their turn. "I was pretty sure he was not going to be there for us," said an Angels scout.

A rookie practices pitching at the Angels' minor-league training field.

Mike and his family went to the MLB Network offices in Secaucus, New Jersey, on June 9 for the draft. They sat and waited as teams picked other players. Then, with the 25th pick, the Angels chose Mike. He was thrilled. "Words can't describe that day," Mike said. He also got to meet some former MLB players. "They treated me like a king."

The Angels put Mike on their rookie team. Most first-year players start on this type of team. Mike proved right away that Los Angeles had made the right decision in the draft. Mike hit .352 in his first 44 games. He also had 13 **stolen bases**.

Mike *(right)* gets tagged out trying to steal second base at the 2010 Futures Game.

Mike *(right)* and his parents at a game against the Oakland Athletics.

Mike moved up to the Class A Cedar Rapids (Iowa) Kernels in 2010. He put up incredible numbers in 81 games with the team. His batting average was .362. He also hit six home runs and stole 46 bases. *Baseball America* and MLB named Mike to the 2010 Futures Game.

The game is a showcase for some of baseball's brightest future stars. "It's really an honor to play in this game," Mike said before taking the field. "I can't wait to get out there."

The young outfielder moved up to Class AA Arkansas Travelers in 2011. This league's tougher competition didn't slow him down. Mike hit .326 in 91 games. He also had 11 home runs and 33 stolen bases.

In early July, the Angels made a big announcement. They called Mike up to the major leagues. Los Angeles manager Mike Scioscia was excited about his newest player. "Mike Trout has a chance to be a special player," Scioscia said. "He has all the tools and the desire to make things happen."

Mike runs the bases in a 2011 game against the Seattle Mariners.

LOS ANGELES SUPERSTAR

Many players struggle after moving up to the major-league level. It is the toughest baseball league in the world. Throughout 2011, Mike didn't play as well in the majors as he'd hoped.

Mike played well in the outfield for the Angels right away.

In 40 games with the Angels, his batting average was just .220. But he did hit five home runs and steal four bases.

The Angels knew that Mike would adjust to MLB with time. "You've got to let him take his bumps and bruises, let him learn the game and learn the league," said former teammate Torii Hunter.

Mike began the 2012 season with the Class AAA Salt Lake Bees. But the Angels quickly called him back up to the majors. This time, Mike took full advantage of his opportunity. He hit for power and stole bases. He made great catches.

MLB fans chose Mike for that year's **All-Star Game**. He got a hit in his first at bat.

Mike hits the ball during the 2012 All-Star Game.

Mike *(right)* steals a base in the sixth inning of the 2012 All-Star Game.

This made Mike the youngest player to get a hit in an All-Star Game since 1955. He also stole a base.

Mike hadn't played many games with the Angels in 2011. So he was still considered a rookie in 2012. He put up one of the greatest rookie seasons in baseball history. Mike hit .326 in 132 games. He also stole 49 bases and hit 30 home runs. Only a few MLB players have put up those combined numbers in one season.

Many people thought Mike should have been named the AL MVP. But the award went to Miguel Cabrera. Mike settled for winning the AL Rookie of the Year award.

Mike appears in TV ads for Subway restaurants. His favorite sub sandwich is an Italian on white bread.

Mike *(right)* slides to beat the tag in a 2013 game against the White Sox.

By the end of the 2012 season, Mike was a superstar. These days, he appears in TV commercials all around the country. Baseball fans everywhere know his name.

Mike continued his hot hitting in 2013. He was selected to his second All-Star Game. But he knows not to take his success for granted. "I'm just happy I got a chance to play pro ball," Mike said.

Mike waves to his fans during a parade before the 2013 All-Star Game.

Selected Career Highlights

2013 Named to second All-Star Game

2012 Won Rookie of the Year award
Named to All-Star Game
Became youngest player in MLB history with at least 30 home runs
  and 30 stolen bases in a season

2011 Called up to Los Angeles Angels for the first time
Named Minor League Player of the Year by *Baseball America*

2010 Named to Futures Game

2009 Changed position from shortstop to outfield
Drafted by the Los Angeles Angels
Named to New Jersey All-State team for the second time

2008 Named to New Jersey All-State team

2007 Pitched and played shortstop on varsity team

2006 Made varsity team as a freshman

Glossary

All-Star Game: a game played in the middle of each season, featuring the top players of the American League and the National League

American League (AL): one of MLB's two leagues. The AL has 15 teams, including the Los Angeles Angels, the Kansas City Royals, the Texas Rangers, and the New York Yankees.

ball boy: a boy who retrieves balls that go out of play

batting average: a number that describes how often a baseball player gets a hit

cycle: hitting a single, a double, a triple, and a home run in the same game

double: a hit that allows a batter to safely reach second base

draft: a yearly event in which teams select high school and college players

dugout: the enclosed area with a long bench along either side of a baseball field. Players and coaches sit or stand in the dugout during a game.

home run: a hit that allows a batter to run all the way around the bases to score a run

linebacker: a football player who usually stays behind the defensive line

minor league: a group of teams in which players gain experience and improve their skills before going to the major leagues

rookie: a first-year player

scout: a person who judges the skills of players

shortstop: a player who plays in the field between second and third base

single: a hit that allows a batter to safely reach first base

stolen bases: when runners advance a base while the pitcher is throwing the ball to home plate

triple: a hit that allows a batter to safely reach third base

varsity: the top sports team at a school

Further Reading & Websites

Fishman, Jon M. *Miguel Cabrera*. Minneapolis: Lerner Publications, 2013.

Kennedy, Mike, and Mark Stewart. *Long Ball: The Legend and Lore of the Home Run*. Minneapolis: Millbrook Press, 2006.

Savage, Jeff. *Stephen Strasburg*. Minneapolis: Lerner Publications, 2013.

The Official Site of Major League Baseball
http://www.mlb.com/home
Major League Baseball's official website provides fans with the latest scores and game schedules, as well as information on players, teams, and baseball history.

The Official Site of the Los Angeles Angels
http://losangeles.angels.mlb.com/index.jsp?c_id=ana
The Los Angeles Angels official site includes the team schedule and game results. Visitors can also find late-breaking news, biographies of Mike Trout and other players and coaches, and much more.

Sports Illustrated Kids
http://www.sikids.com
The *Sports Illustrated Kids* website covers all sports, including baseball.

LERNER

SOURCE

Expand learning beyond the printed book. Download free, complementary educational resources for this book from our website, www.lerneresource.com.

Index

Photo Acknowledgments

The images in this book are used with the permission of: AP Photo/Rob Carmell/CSM (Cal Sport Media), p. 4; © Harry How/Getty Images, p. 5, 6, 29; AP Photo/Alex Gallardo, p. 7; © Ed Zurga/Stringer/Getty Images, p. 9; © R. Nelson/Getty Images, p. 10; Seth Poppel Yearbook Library, p. 11, 14, 15, 16; © Doug Kerr, p. 12; © Jeff Greeenberg/Alamy, p. 18; © Kevin Sullivan/Orange County Register/Alamy, p. 19; © Michael Goulding/Zumapress/Newscom, p. 20; © Deanne Fitzmaurice/Sports Illustrated/Getty Images, p. 21; © Otto Greule Jr./Getty Images, p. 23; © Thearon W. Henderson/Getty Images, p. 24; AP Photo/Charlie Neibergall, p. 25; AP Photo/Jeff Roberson, p. 26; © Jonathan Daniel/Getty Images, p. 27; © Thomas Levison/Stringer/Getty Images, p. 28.

Front cover: Otto Greule Jr/Getty Images.

Main body text set in Caecilia LT Std 55 Roman 16/28.
Typeface provided by Adobe Systems.